PHONICS CHAPTER BOOK 6

A Bag of Tricks

Folk Tales From Around the World

as retold by
Yoko Mia Hirano
Jesús Cervantes
Angela Shelf Medearis
Iai Lay
Janelle Cherrington
Felix Pitre

**Illustrated by
Kathleen Kuchera**

Scholastic Inc.
New York   Toronto   London   Auckland   Sydney

Copyright © 1998 by Scholastic Inc.
Scholastic *Phonics Chapter Books* is a trademark of Scholastic Inc.
All rights reserved. Published by Scholastic Inc.
Printed in the U.S.A.
ISBN 0-590-76458-6
5 6 7 8 9 10   14   04 03 02 01 00 99 98

Dear Teacher/Family Member,

Research has shown that phonics is an essential strategy for figuring out unknown words. Early readers need the opportunity to learn letter sounds and how to blend or put them together to make words. These skills must be practiced over and over again by reading stories containing words with the sounds being taught.

That's why I'm happy to be an author and Program Coordinator of the **Phonics Chapter Books**. These books provide early readers with playful, fanciful stories in easy-to-manage chapters. More importantly, the words in the stories are controlled for phonics sounds and common sight words. Once sounds and sight words have been introduced, they are continually reviewed and applied in succeeding stories, so children will be able to decode these books—and read them on their own. There is nothing more powerful and encouraging than success.

John Shefelbine
Associate Professor, Reading Education
California State University, Sacramento

CONTENTS

How the Crocodile Was Fooled

1

Once upon a time there lived a rabbit on a little island in Japan. This rabbit had never set foot off the island, and she was bored. She wanted more room to hop around.

Now, this rabbit was no fool. She saw that getting off the island would be a problem. She could not swim, and she had no wood to make a boat. She waited for the day something would happen to help her get off the island.

That day came soon. The rabbit was
on the beach looking at the sea. It was
noon and the sun was hot, so she stood
in the cool, damp sand.

All of a sudden she saw a big crocodile!
The rabbit was about to hop away, when
the crocodile said, "Good day!"

The crocodile was in a good mood. "Look, I am not a crook," he said. "Come. I just want to chat."

So the rabbit and the crocodile spoke about many things. Soon the rabbit got an idea. She said, "Don't you have any crocodile friends to chat with?"

"I have many friends," said the crocodile in a huff.

"Do you have so many friends that they could line up from this beach all the way to the mainland?" the rabbit asked.

The crocodile said, "Yes. I will show you!"

So the crocodile got his friends to line up, side by side, all the way to the mainland.

"You do have a lot of friends," said the rabbit. "Just let me count each crocodile as I hop on its back."

Then the rabbit jumped, foot by foot,
from the back of one crocodile to
the next, all the way to the mainland.

The rabbit called to the crocodile,
"I fooled you and your friends to help
me get to the mainland. Ha, ha, ha!"

The crocodile was sad.
"Come back!" he yelled.

But the rabbit was
so happy to be on
the loose, she did not
look back even once.

2 Frog Tricks Loud Rabbit

There once was a rabbit who could run very fast. He liked to go to the hilltop and brag to all the town about his swift speed. "I can run the fastest!" he would shout out loud.

Then Frog came along. Rabbit's loud boasting made him mad. He went up to Rabbit and said, "No one wants to hear this racket! I will race you down to the pond, and I will win!"

"Let's race now!" said Rabbit.

"No," said Frog. "You run outside on the ground a lot, and I do not. I need two days to practice."

Rabbit said that was fine. He even let Frog choose where they would race. Frog said they should race in the tall swamp grass, from the hill down to the pond.

Frog went to count how many hops it took to get from the hill to the pond. Then he went back to his little brown house in the ground. He had planned a trick.

On the day of the race, Rabbit and Frog were set to go. Frog was about to play his trick. He had asked all of his frog friends to hide in the thick swamp grass. The frogs were lined up, each frog one good leap from the next.

The race began. Rabbit ran as fast as he could. Soon, at a bend in the road, he saw a frog jump out of the grass in front of him. After that, the next frog jumped out, then the next, all the way down to the pond.

Rabbit was thinking it was Frog who was always one jump in front of him. So Rabbit ran faster and faster. In the end it was Frog who was waiting at the pond for Rabbit.

Rabbit was running too fast to stop. He fell into the pond just as Frog shouted as loud as he could, "I am the fastest!"

And that was that.

3 Sister Hen's Cool Drink

One afternoon Hen went down by the creek, looking for a cool drink.

Hen drank and drank. She did not hear Crocodile as he came swimming up to her.

In a loud tone Crocodile said, "Stop drinking from my creek, or I will eat you up!"

My, oh my! Hen ran from Crocodile as fast as she could.

But Crocodile came slinking after her. He grabbed her tail.

"Please don't eat me, brother!" Hen said.

My, oh my! When Hen called Crocodile "brother," it made his jaws drop open. So, quick as a wink, Hen yanked her tail out and ran away. She did not stop running until she was safe in her nest.

14

"My, oh my!" Crocodile was thinking. "Why did Hen call me her brother?"

He slinked off the muddy bank into the creek. Kaplunk!

Crocodile could not think why Hen would call him "brother." He did not have feet like Hen. Hen did not have teeth like Crocodile.

He was still thinking about it the next day when Hen came down from her nest for a cool drink from the creek.

"Stop!" said Crocodile, slinking up next to her. "I want to ask you something."

"What is it?" Hen said. This time she was not afraid.

"Why did you call me your brother? I was thinking and thinking about it, but I do not get it," Crocodile said. "You are small and I am big. You are black and I am green. How can I be your brother?"

"Because," said Hen, "you come from an egg, and I come from an egg. So we must be family."

"Thank you," said Crocodile. "In that case, I guess I can't eat you after all."

Then Crocodile slinked off the muddy bank into the creek. Kaplunk!

4 How Possum Asked for His Skinny Tail

In the old days Possum had the most beautiful tail of all. Each day he stood and flicked his big, silky tail this way and that as he showed it off.

Possum brushed and fussed over his tail all the time, but he liked it most when the other animals looked on. Possum, you see, was very vain.

It was Rabbit who planned to teach Possum a lesson. Rabbit called on Possum and asked him to come to the next town meeting.

"Chief Bear insisted that you sit next to him at the meeting. He wants you to give a speech because you have the most beautiful tail," Rabbit said.

Possum said he would go. It was then that Rabbit told Possum he had some mud on his tail.

"I will be happy to clean it for you," said Rabbit as he grabbed some liquid from his bag.

Rabbit rubbed the liquid all over Possum's tail, then put an old snakeskin around it. Rabbit told Possum to leave the snakeskin on until it was time for him to speak at the meeting.

The next day when all the animals were seated at the meeting, Possum jumped up and took off the snakeskin. He posed to best show off his tail, but the animals began to laugh. Some even shouted, "Ugly! Ugly!"

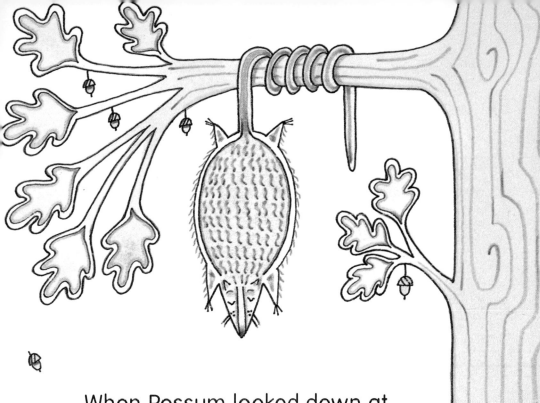

When Possum looked down at his tail, he saw that it was bald. Possum was so ashamed! He waited until all the animals had left, then rushed to the tree branch where he lived.

Even today Possum hangs upside down in a tree to sleep, for that is the one good thing he can do with his bald, ugly tail.

21

5 Sly Gretel

Once upon a time a cook named Gretel worked for the town mayor. One day the mayor said, "Gretel, please fry up your fine cheese fritters for tonight. I am expecting a guest."

Gretel got right to work. She grated the cheese, added the spices, shaped the fritters, and dropped them in a pan to fry. Soon they were nice and brown, and they smelled oh so good! Yet, Gretel could not set them out, because the guest had not come.

"It is such a shame they can't be eaten now," Gretel said with a sigh. "They are hot, and they look just right, but one can't always tell by looking. Maybe I should try just one little bite."

First, she cut a thick slice from the fritter on top and ate it up. "Oh my, that is good," she said. "But the thing does look quite a sight with that big slice cut out. I should eat the rest of it right up."

Soon Gretel had eaten a second fritter. She called to the mayor to ask if his guest had come.

"Not yet," was the mayor's reply.

"Why, these fritters are getting cold," Gretel said to herself. "I can't drop them back in the pan, or they will get cooked to a crisp. Maybe the guest will not show up at all. I may as well eat one more fritter while they are still hot."

As soon as Gretel had eaten that one, she had to try one more to see if it was just as good. It was.

Soon, Gretel had popped the very last fritter on the plate right into her mouth!

As Gretel wiped her chin dry, the mayor called, "Gretel, I think my guest might be coming up the path."

"Okay," said Gretel. "I will bring the food out in a moment."

Just then the guest came to the back door by mistake. Gretel opened it up a crack and said, "Run away, run away! The mayor is very upset that you are late!"

The man was frightened. "Thank you," he said as he ran back down the path.

Then Gretel called to the mayor, "Mayor, your guest just took my fritters and is running away with them!"

"Did he not leave even one little bite for me?" the mayor asked.

The sly Gretel said, "No. He took them all, but I will make some more right away."

6 How the Kind Beetle Got Her Coat

In the lush green jungle of old, a slow gray beetle walked across the ground. She was minding her own business when she ran into a wild gray rat.

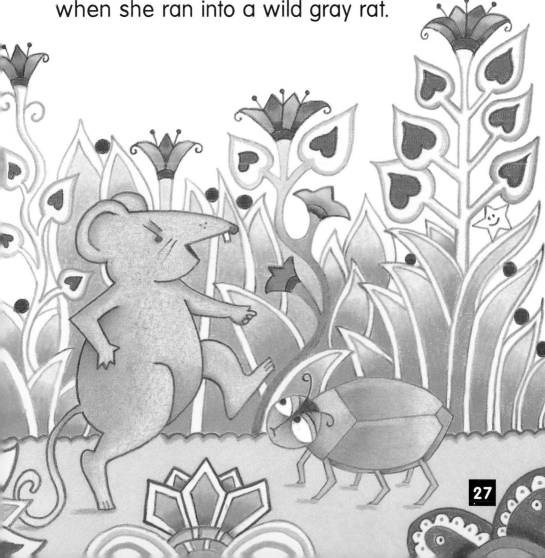

The rat was very fast and mean. He stood up on his hind legs and said, "Look at you, you old beetle. You are so slow. Don't you wish you could be fast like me?" The rat liked to make fun of the slow beetle.

The mild little beetle did not wish to fight with the rat. She just nodded, and she did not tell him about the many things she could do if she wanted.

A wise parrot in a tree could hear the wild rat and the quiet little beetle. After a while the parrot said to himself, "I just bet that beetle has some trick up her sleeve. What might it be?"

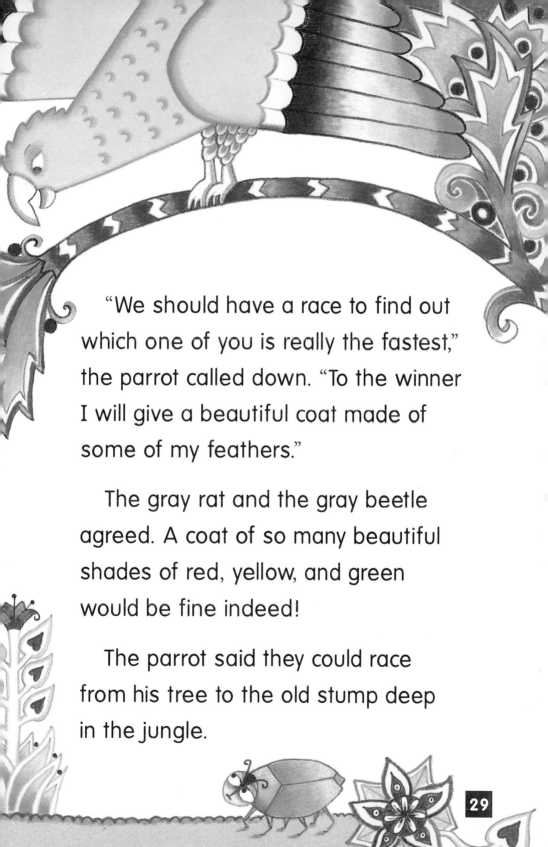

"We should have a race to find out which one of you is really the fastest," the parrot called down. "To the winner I will give a beautiful coat made of some of my feathers."

The gray rat and the gray beetle agreed. A coat of so many beautiful shades of red, yellow, and green would be fine indeed!

The parrot said they could race from his tree to the old stump deep in the jungle.

29

When the parrot yelled "GO!"
the rat pumped his thick hind legs
and ran and ran. He was fast, but he
reached the stump only to find that
the kind beetle was there.

"How did you win?" asked the rat.

"I used my wings," said the beetle as
she tucked them away. "You see, I can
go very fast when I have a mind to do it."

That is why today beetles have
beautiful coats and wild rats are still
dull and gray.

Folk Tales From Around the World

Folk tales are some of the oldest stories told to children. Many of the same stories have been passed from country to country. The stories in this book are all about playing tricks. Some are funny, some teach a lesson, and some explain how something came to be. Children all over the world like to read folk tales, and we hope you liked reading these.

PHONICS

Decodable Words With the Phonic Elements

1 ōō crook   ōō cool
      foot   fool
      good   loose
      look   mood
      stood   noon
      wood   room
               soon

2 ou out   ow brown
      outside   down
      about   town
      count   now
      ground
      house
      loud
      shout

3 -ank bank
      drank
      thank
      yanked

    -ing drinking
      looking
      running
      slinking
      something
      swimming
      thinking

    -ink drink
      slinked
      think
      wink

    -unk kaplunk

4 -ed /d/ ashamed   /t/ asked
      called   brushed
      grabbed   flicked
      lived   fussed
      planned   jumped
      posed   liked
      rubbed   looked
      showed   rushed

    /ed/ insisted
      seated
      shouted
      waited

5 y by   igh sigh
    dry   -ight frightened
    fry   might
    my   right
    reply   sight
    sly   tonight
    try
    why

6 -ild mild
      wild

    -ind find
      hind
      kind
      mind